my stay with the sisters
poems

Cheryl Cantafio

D1596531

ISBN 979-8-9880452-0-5 (paperback)
ISBN 979-8-9880452-1-2 (e-book)

Cover & illustrations by Olivia L. Sutton

Edited by Shelby Leigh

Printed in the United States of America.

Content warning: Cancer, Death, Death of a Loved One

For Mom,
waves hello
I miss you.

For Dad,
who welcomed me into this world
with a poem.

contents

introduction

My Mom lost her battle with metastatic pancreatic cancer in April 2022. And while cancer took her from us, it did not define who she was. She was 74 years young, a loving wife of 52 years, a mom, a gigi (grandmother), a sister, an aunt, a friend, and a woman who had more living to do.

Family and friends have been kind and supportive and loving. But, there were many moments when her loss felt unbearable. All I wanted to do was find a place to cry, scream, sleep, remember good times and special moments, breathe, and return to life as a functioning human being. This feeling was—and is—on a loop.

Enter the sisters and their home.

my stay with the sisters was a way to find my words and to get some of the pain out, especially when all I felt like doing was nothing or ugly cry if someone said hello to me.

Throughout this book, you'll see Grief and Gratitude—sisters who are well-meaning friends. They are erratic. They are cathartic. And bless them (in their own weird ways) they're trying to help.

I imagined them welcoming me into their home and offering rooms for me to use as I needed them.

I welcome you now to turn the page and to meet Grief and Gratitude. They invite you, as they did me, to find comfort. To feel less alone. Think of their home as a vacation rental for when you really need to let loose.

I placed poems about my experiences with loss in the rooms of their home.

Feel free to visit whichever room speaks to you. Consider it a choose-your-own poetry experience. I hope you feel less alone here if you are mourning or missing someone.

xo,
Cher

meet the sisters

we are the sisters
Grief and Gratitude

we are the sisters Grief and Gratitude.
one is the storm; the other is the calm.
if you can't accept us both, loss is skewed.

with a loss of this magnitude,
we know. go ahead—scream that f-bomb.
we are the sisters Grief and Gratitude.

Gratitude often soothes the mood.
succumbing to Grief requires calming balm.
if you can't accept us both, loss is skewed.

Grief is demanding—she's less subdued.
Gratitude is there to catch tears in her palm.
we are the sisters Grief and Gratitude.

Grief is a storm, a continuous brood.
she feels like an internal ticking time bomb.
if you can't accept us both, loss is skewed.

Grief allows rage, Gratitude allows quietude.
the duo fit together—hand in glove.
we are the sisters Grief and Gratitude.
if you can't accept us both, loss is skewed.

a note from Grief

i know i can be erratic
during a time that is traumatic.
please don't think i'm being dramatic;
i don't really have a schematic.
when i visit isn't always pragmatic,
but that's how i work with Gratitude
among Sorrow's noise and static.

a note from Gratitude

hello, dear friend.
when Sorrow feels difficult to transcend,
let your good memories ascend.
i promise that if you smile you won't offend.
if there's any advice i can lend,
let joy and kindness help you mend.

welcome to the house

the sisters' home awaits

welcome! come on in.
don't worry about making
a mess. this house is
lived in, each room a place of
solace, ready for your use.

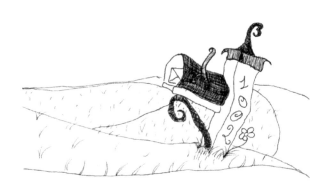

the conservatory

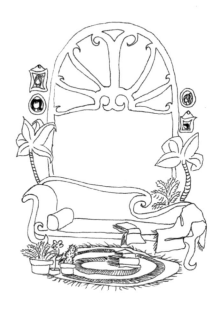

a sanctuary
sunlight, books, music, chaise lounge,
an eclectic hug,
an orientation point,
a room to get lost or found.

left behind

we are the people left behind.
Death came (*too soon? in time?*) for you;
love and memories are the ties that bind.

Dad was loving devotion defined,
your every need always attended to.
we are the people left behind.

your youngest provided peace of mind.
worked magic for you to pass through.
love and memories are the ties that bind.

your granddaughter is a light, one-of-a-kind.
how she misses you.
we are the people left behind.

your friends stood by you, sad, resigned.
you have quite a crew.
love and memories are the ties that bind.

countless others loved you, bear in mind.
i can only hope i do right by you.
we are the people left behind.
love and memories are the ties that bind.

51 days

it's been 51 days.
i get out of bed at dawn.
i stare at 50 in the mirror and i'm in a haze.

a milestone birthday gone sideways.
how can it be happy when you're gone?
it's been 51 days.

how heavy all of this weighs.
well wishes—*i know it's hard*—and so on.
i stare at 50 in the mirror and i'm in a haze.

oh goodie, more grays.
time for retail therapy—thanks, Amazon.
it's been 51 days.

Mom loved celebrating birthdays.
she was robbed of her 75th so i carry on.
i stare at 50 in the mirror and i'm in a haze.

i hope for us there are many more birthdays,
so i smile, eat tiramisu, withdraw less.
it's been 51 days.
i stare at 50 in the mirror and i'm in a haze.

meet the sisters' extended brood

since you've met Grief and Gratitude,
they've invited their family to join us, too.
it's time to meet their extended brood.

Sorrow you know—she darkens the mood.
the tears and pain flow; you'll need a tissue,
since you've met Grief and Gratitude.

there's Rage and Ire, brothers so crude.
it's delicious, the wrath they brew.
it's time to meet their extended brood.

Confusion whispers, *something's skewed.*
past and present tenses feel like a miscue
since you've met Grief and Gratitude.

Resentment and Envy are a prelude
to ruining holidays. they are your clue.
it's time to meet their extended brood.

Hope offers quietude.
it carries on, the love you knew,
since you've met Grief and Gratitude,
since you've met their extended brood.

i'd like to report a time robbery

another ten years,
that's what you both thought you had.
i can't stop my tears.

smoke

evade with *i'm fine*;
obfuscate with a small smile;
confuse by laughing.

they know

your furry friends know,
maybe before you do, how
much you need their love.

i don't know what to wish for

get up, feed the dogs,
start my workday, break for lunch.
ah. it's five o'clock.
what's for dinner? more takeout.
shower, kiss my love goodnight.

and we rinse, repeat.
rinse. repeat. rinse. repeat.
rinse the sorrow away.
just like the unexpected,
routine can be a blessing.

movement

moving fast and slow,
          from erratic to static—
now where do i go?
                    pause,
                         stop,
                              fast forward,

     rewind.

my sixth sense is off-kilter.

someone help me out here

is it too soon
to feel joy, happy, or silly?
is it too soon
to resume guilt-free normalcy?
i can't shake the sadness yet.

the sisters have no rhythm or rhyme

the sisters have no rhythm, no rhyme.
i need to keep it together. please—*not now!*
ladies, please—maybe another time?

sometimes they move double-time.
i remember how my parents danced. *wow.*
the sisters have no rhythm, no rhyme.

this emotional rollercoaster is a crime.
Mom loved a good thriller. *zap! pow!*
ladies, please—maybe another time?

when i receive spring flowers—sublime!
Mom looked great in that color! *yow!*
the sisters have no rhythm, no rhyme.

i just burst into tears at the store big-time.
bravo, sisters. slow clap. *take a bow.*
ladies, please—maybe another time?

one day it's better, the next it's slime.
today a smile, tomorrow a furrowed brow.
the sisters have no rhythm, no rhyme.
ladies, please—some other time.

echo

you are solid and you are an echo.

you are solid and you are an echo.

wish for more of you here, less echo.

wish for more of you here, less echo.

you reverberate in our hearts.

you reverberate in our hearts.

there's so much more to share.

there's so much more to share.

i wish we could know.

i wish we could know.

are we echoes to you?

are we echoes to you?

love you and miss you.

love you and miss you.

love you.

awkward

i opened my mouth,
and *my mother is gone* fell out.

well…really, it tumbled.

        i stumbled

           i bumbled

               i crumbled

                  i fumbled

i tried to recover but it came out all jumbled.

succumbing to my tears at the store
i mumbled,

i'll just show myself out…

i forgot to ask

i never thought to
ask Mom what she envisioned
heaven would be like.
i'm pissed off at myself.
i'd like her version in my head.

tongue-tied

i'm an open book
with friends and sometimes strangers.
Mom's story spills free;
other times my tongue won't move.
what the hell is wrong with me?

worst timepiece ever

there's more behind me
than ahead, and my life's watch
won't tell exact time.
i cannot set an alarm
to finish the life i started.

lean harder

i should have leaned harder
into being in photos;
i should have leaned harder
into taking you to Rockettes shows;
i should have leaned harder
into staying with you at the shore.
i should have leaned harder
because i can't anymore.

perspective

friends losing parents
hits differently—harder now.
like losing you twice.

anxiety, table for two

why am i anxious?
oh, right. we said goodbye here.
i've tried to steer clear
of the final place you were
lying in state. life goes on.

why am i anxious?
worst-case scenarios plague
every waking thought.
i wait for bad to happen.
but it doesn't. life goes on.

why am i anxious?
oh, no. one little mistake
and my mind spirals.
i've made myself small again.
i recover. life goes on.

why am i anxious?
Anxiety, please depart.
i cannot control
what happens. i never could.
i struggle to accept that life goes on.

after

after your farewell,
i did not think i'd fare well.
it felt like pure hell,
like i was under a spell,
and the antidote was lost.

mom's the word

i envy those who
are able to call their moms
and hear their voices.
mom is the word left on the string
that connected our tin cans.

signs, signs, nowhere a sign

i need a big sign.
nothing subtle like red birds.
let me know you're fine.
drop me a hint, like houses
that fall on wicked witches.

my stay with the sisters   41

the rage room

the room's all yours

feeling your anger grow?
ready to issue a counterblow?
do you want something to throw?
use this room to let the rage flow.

scream! wail! bellow!
here—smash this old banjo!

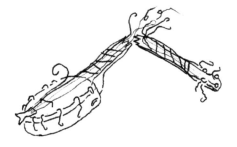

demolish the dishes with gusto!
hit the punching bag with a one-two combo!

doesn't it feel good to let it all go?

things will never be the same

things will never be the same.
someone said your passing would be a
gentle tap on the shoulder;
my world was set aflame.

the last time i heard Mom say my name,
i choked on the words i wanted to tell her.
things will never be the same.

cancer played a cruel, quick endgame.
that gentle tap? *pffft*—it hit like a boulder.
my world was set aflame.

she rests in peace, in our hearts, a picture frame.
i can never again hug or hold her.
things will never be the same.

old home movies unlock frame by frame;
others are lost in my brain (a faulty memory
holder).
my world was set aflame.

as i claw my way out of sorrow,
heartbreak, shame—
feelings erupt, retreat, smolder.
things will never be the same.
my world was set aflame.

diagnosis

you're kidding me, right?
the phone burns hot in my hand;
i am ill-prepared.
Mom survived a pandemic,
but cancer wants to claim her?

predator

you have hunted us
throughout our generations.
your newest arrow,
pancreatic cancer, wounds.
i hope you choke on chemo.

sucker-punched and prickly

have you noticed it?
one person dies, another
six awful events
sprout up? enough already!
give us all a damned minute.

i'd *love* to know the reason

things happen for a
reason is total bullshit.
shut up. just stop it.

extroverts knock me out

how do you do that?
you, unlawful chaotic.
what magic is this?
i'm exhausted watching you—
maybe a little jealous.

let's make some noise

sometimes the quiet
rattles my cage, irritates
me into seeking
the hubbub, energy, and
solace of a raucous night.

it's a shock every. single. time.

the hard truth of it:
we are stone-cold idiots.

time TICKS,

         TiCkS,

                  Ticks,

                            ticks,

in the blink of an eye
we are breathing in sea air,
then standing at the horizon of the afterlife.
and yet we remain surprised
when our ferryman arrives.

outside voice

i use my polite voice meant for outside;
true reactions locked away in a cage.
otherwise, people would be horrified.

i'm not always dry-eyed
as expected (or sage).
i use my polite voice meant for outside.

the voice inside my head would open wide,
but i curtail my devastation and rage.
otherwise, people would be horrified.

i let things that piss me off slide.
(it's not worth it at this stage.)
i use my polite voice meant for outside.

they gave us false hope—they lied!
i resist writing my true feelings on a page.
otherwise, people would be horrified.

it's a balance of Jekyll and Hyde
(but my face betrays a lack of courage).
i use my polite voice meant for outside.
otherwise, people would be horrified.

minx

Death is mischievous,
almost a low-key Loki—
he hides the punchlines.

i'm not having it

let's talk great beyond.
unpopular opinion:
       it isn't that great,
            and beyond isn't that far.
look for another lodestar.

requiem for a squeam

i am composing
a requiem for my squeams.
i have let my qualms
be my guide, and all for what?
time to take up space and live.

your death left me numb struck

a numbing moment
when it's all said and done,
your mortal coil shed.
all that's left are memories.

thanks, hate the shedding.

wish you were here.

tissue alert

i should probably
warn you when you kindly ask,
how are you doing?
i reply with words and tears.
please don't mind me—i'm leaky.

the entertainment room

you can sit with us

enjoy the flicker
of home movies on the screen.
reminisce a bit,
curl up with a warm blanket,
and hold dear to the good times.

she needed something

she needed something to feel like long ago.
off to the movies Mom and Dad went.
merci, Monsieur Poirot.

excited to be somewhere, no rules to follow.
the theater to themselves, time well spent.
she needed something to feel like long ago.

the mystery unfolds—the screen is aglow.
something is suspect with that gent!
merci, Monsieur Poirot.

the setting is Egypt, a trip they had to forego
due to the pandemic, much to their lament.
she needed something to feel like long ago.

how does he deduce who is friend or foe?
Mom knew that person wasn't so innocent.
merci, Monsieur Poirot.

what a wonderful movie—what a show!
that time together worth every cent.
she needed something to feel like long ago.
merci, Monsieur Poirot.

visiting Cindy's home

time at the castle
will forever be cherished.
wish we could be there.

beach, please!

Mom placed her
chair and toes in the ocean,
and it welcomed her.

rebellion

rebel Mom captured
in a single black-and-white
photograph—shock-white-
blonde hair, bold cat's-eye makeup—
a fierce look that screams *try me.*

give her all the books

mysteries,
histories,
memoirs,
suspense,
historical fiction,
regency romance,
biographies, too.

Mom was enthralled with so many books.

ticket to dream

picture it—center city 1953.
a young girl sat in
her first movie theater.
fly, imagination, fly.

loads of modes to roads

planes, helicopters,
Paris, England, Hawaii,
trains, cars, and cruises,
Switzerland, Monaco, more.
bird of passage, how you soared.

shenanigans

all we had to do
was look at each other.
side eye, eye rolls, brows
furrowed. one more look, warning
us—*do not make me laugh now.*

when Grief picks the movie

Gratitude pours the wine
as Grief starts the movie.

what are we going to watch?

Grief beams.

old yeller!

what's with the face?

look! a dog.

inheritance

i inherited
her fondness for reading books—
any tome with a
suspect, weapon, place, motives,
flawed detectives, and their crooks.

laughing at inappropriate moments

uh oh

the weirdest thoughts pop into my head.

giggle

and then my cheeks turn cherry-red.

snicker

this is poor timing—i wish i was stronger

snort

but i can't hold it in any longer,

cackle

and the noise i make

bahahahaha!

reverberates like an earthquake.

dancing with

Gratitude and Grief

Gratitude dances
a smile across my face.
today was better.

Grief threw me into
a mosh pit—the music loud,
seething. i felt stronger.

her name is Sally

when i hear her name
in a movie or a song,
i smile all day long.

Gratitude, the musical

a core memory:
traveling with you to see
my first musical
about a chance at Broadway.
i wished Zach could pick them all.

birth year

i wonder if you
knew *the music in my heart*
opened on your first
day of life. it seems you were
destined to love theater.

hey, Ang

hey, Ang. heard the news.
dear lady, you were so loved.
maybe you and Mom
can solve some real mysteries
beyond the Cove of Cabot.

sit down, Billy

the Bard lied to us.
he made death seem romantic.
we do not leave on
iambic pentameter.
it's more free verse, less sonnet.

the kitchen

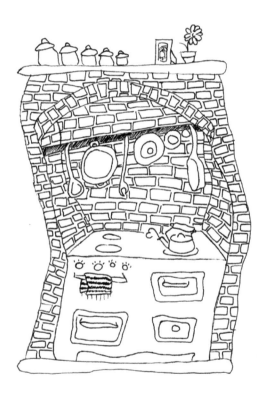

the kitchen

stop by the kitchen
for a meal or cup of tea.
supper's better than
that big bowl of emotions
you are trying to swallow.

reunion

i would love to crash
your family reunion.
Grandmom's warm embrace;
Grandpop's homemade chicken soup.
you. happy and whole again.

debugging loss

Guilt is eavesdropping,
relentless, a parasite
waiting to devour
every twisted thought you have.

don't give her a single bite.

birthday girl

October baby.
beautiful Libra.
year seventy-five.
year of the diamond.

in our hearts you are
blowing out candles,
planning your next trip,
laughing with Daddy.

October baby.
beautiful Libra.
we're here wondering
did you make a wish?

scents from an Italian restaurant

i turned the corner
and the memories poured in.
my olfactory
senses brought you back to me,
entering that restaurant.

the mourner's hug mug
(concocted by the sisters)

warm up a mug
pour a finger of bourbon
or brandy
(or cognac)

add
a little honey
a few splashes of bitters
(bitters build balance)

squeeze
fresh lemon juice
or orange juice
(*whichever makes your taste buds happiest*)

boil some tea
add it to the magic in your mug
stir it together

add some spice
star anise
maybe nutmeg
(cloves are nice)

sip it down
feel its warmth
let it envelop you
(enjoy its comfort)

cookie press

of all the cookies
i will miss this year
i think i will miss
the cookie press ones
the most, because we
had ourselves a good laugh at
making a mess out
of the first attempts.

i will miss that mess.

hello? is this thing on?

universe, you there?
i hope you can hook me up
with a little spark,
enlightenment, or brilliance.
i am all out of matches.

mourning magnet

i shower and dress for a happy occasion.
i do a sniff check— make sure
i don't reek of Sad.

and yet
     and yet
          and yet—

i am found.
i attract them.
i am a magnet to the others.

those still mourning their losses.
those seeking to share loved ones' stories.
those who don't know why they're spilling
their guts to me but can't stop.

it was lovely while it lasted.
i wish i hadn't been found.
i wish i hadn't attracted them.
i wish i could repel the others.

and yet
         and yet
                  and yet—

we still need to feel, to mourn.
we still need to find solace—it hurts.
we still need to spill our guts.

i get it.
i am drawn to them, too.
i shove cake into my mouth, listen, and hope
we can make sense of it all.

the bedroom

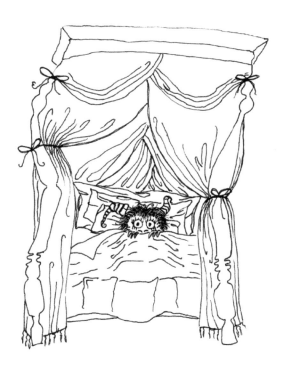

bed is calling me

sometimes it feels like
the only place that provides
refuge is bed.
soft covers protect us from
an emotional maelstrom.

why is there a monster in my room?

the bedroom has all you will need for the
night:

> pajamas and a robe
>
> a turned-down bed
>
> soft mattress
>
> lots of pillows
>
> a nightlight to find your way

and one monster.
(he prefers you call him Angus.)

he is there in case you need:

> a hug in the middle of the night,
>
> a protector from the nightmares,
>
> a tissue to wipe away the tears,
>
> a glass of water,
>
> a good listener for your memories.

witness to Mom's last rites

what did the priest say?
my brain will not allow me
any solace here.

let her sleep

dear friend Death arrived,
and Mom was waiting, ready.
they walked by the couch.

Death observed me, sleeping soundly.
Mom squeezed his hand.

let her sleep.

he's here (whatever that means)

he said, *hey, i'm here.*
where? i'm lost in the before.
in a fog. numb.

the drop-by

listen carefully
to what happens in dreams.
she is visiting.

happy feels weird

happy feels like an
old pair of jeans you put on,
surprised they still fit.

go to sleep, go to sleep, go to sleep

at 2 a.m. is when i wonder,
what's the next thing i'm going to blunder?

my emotions are off the charts.
did you know the octopus has three hearts?

why was that person in my dream?
man, i could go for some ice cream.

i need to go food shopping.
if i don't get up to pee, there's no stopping.

why
are
you
awake?

brain,
please
take
a
break!

quiet

i need quiet.
please, try it.
or i might riot.
and then you'll know some bloody noise.

magic hour

it's magic hour.
sleep turns into dreams,
and i hope i run into you
to tell you all the family gossip.

reflections

you look just like her!
i often wondered if you
found that comforting,
or if you thought, *dear heavens!*
did i really look like that?

mirror, mirror in my head

mirror, mirror in my head.
what's the matter?
i wish i could get rid of this sense of dread!

mirror, mirror, do you see this bedhead?
yeah, that hair is nothing to flatter.
mirror, mirror in my head.

mirror, mirror, i feel like a dunderhead.
remain calm. don't prattle on—don't natter.
i wish i could get rid of this sense of dread!

mirror, mirror, i'm seeing red.
stay cool—any more rage and you'll shatter!
mirror, mirror in my head!

mirror, mirror, where's the plot thread?
quiet your mind before thoughts scatter.
i wish i could get rid of this sense of dread!

girl, wake up! anxiety is a nightmare hotbed.
squash the inner doomsday chatter.
mirror, mirror in my head!
i wish i could get rid of this sense of dread!

reconnect

how long was i gone?
hibernating in my head,
clinging to the pain.
i am slowly waking up,
and trying to reconnect.

you wanna know what scares me?

i am not afraid
of putting in the hard work.

i am not afraid
of tiny imperfections
or others' misperceptions.

i am not afraid
of round two, or three, or four.

i am not afraid
of finishing my milestone,
exclaiming it is complete!

i am afraid
you will never know my work.

i am afraid
it will be a meaningless
legacy, done and dusted.

oh, how i wish

i wish i could tell
you there's a quick, painless way
to mourn, say goodbye.
oh, how i wish. how i wish.
but your hurt is singular.

groggy meditation

do you ever wake
and wonder if this is it?
is it a nightmare?
or is it a life well-lived?
until tomorrow, dear friend.

the garden

a playdate in the dirt

get your hands dirty,
whether you kill plastic plants
or have two green thumbs.
the garden is a space to
practice patience, care, and growth.

take up space

sister Grief can take
up all your headspace; don't
get lost—remember
who you are and that you need

s p a c e to b r e a t h e ,

        walk,

                move *forward*.

birdwatching with the sisters

look, a cardinal!
Gratitude exclaims, giddy.
that wee little bird
reminds me of family!

Grief shrugs.
it's a fucking bird.

jardin de curé

among the flowers,
plants, and shrubbery, there are
color tapestries
of vibrant herbs and robust
vegetation to mend us.

park it here

when you are weary,
you can always rely on
a perfectly placed
wooden bench to take a rest
and reflect on how you've grown.

the sisters attend a funeral

the sisters arrive
and reflect on the pictures,
paving the path to
loved ones who are worn and shell-shocked
with kind words, embraces, and tears.

the eulogy speaks
of both Gratitude and Grief.
sisters bear witness
to legacy, your impact
to family and friends.

the sisters hold them
up, even as their hearts fall.
rest now, rest now, rest.
the sisters will take care of
everything at your request.

reflections ii

when you tell people
your mother died, and they say,
mine too, you can see
your loss mirrored in their eyes.
you're less lonely, yet still alone.

when the ghosts come out to play

it's spooky season.
Halloween, Days of the Dead.
the spell is broken.
i smile at—and mourn—costumed *angelitos*
and angels.

it gets better, right?

sometimes i feel guilty for laughing.
sometimes i feel like feeling n o t h i n g.
sometimes i forget you're gone, and then i
mourn you all over again.
sometimes i want to know what lies beyond.
sometimes i need to know it gets better.

it does, right?
right?

this inquiring mind wants to know

i have questions.
what happens when
we've taken our last breath?

are we
really dead?
is that really it?

from dust
to dust
and all that?

compost for the next generation
to grow,
build on,
and flourish?

or do we continue?

is there a death transport station?
are there boats that take us to our next
destination?

who are the death transporters?
do they play poker
after their shifts?

i have questions.
so many questions.

helicopter child

long day is code for
*i'm dealing with her loss in
my own way today.
give me the space and the grace
i need to do so, okay?*

i am an organic process

i must confess
i'm a bit of a mess.
it might be stress,
>*bless*

>> but i guess
>> some distress
>> helps progress.
>> *unless*

i start to regress.
i need to manifest and express
i'm a work in process,
>*impress*

>> more or less,
>> i will be the authoress
>> of my success.
>>> *yes!*

vocal range

it's so strange
even now, even still,
that your actual voice is out of range.
the silence is so shrill.

you have one new message

i do not know why,
but i checked phone messages.
your name was bolded.
an unanswered message blinks.

> *hi, it's Mom, give me a call.*

i call to the sky,

> *so good to hear from you, Mom.*

i look upward, smile.
even though it's not the same,
i enjoyed our chat today.

please don't leave

Grief and Gratitude,
please don't leave me here alone
with all of my thoughts.
i can't handle another
hole, another void, right now.

the goodie bag

parting gifts

adieu, our dear friend.
thank you for spending time here.
take the goodie bag.
it includes a set of keys.
come and visit anytime.

what would you do?

what would you do
if you knew your time was due?

get up on that stage and sing!
travel to the Maldives and go snorkeling!

savor every dessert on the menu!
book your favorite party venue!

write that memoir!
wish upon a star!

watch the sunset!
waste no time on regret!

tell people you love them!

no, really. don't wait.
tell them you love them
before it's too late.

say yes

if friends invite you,
accept that offer, say *yes.*
your inside voice may
whisper, *no. maybe next time.*
roar back. tell it to say less.

life is about fun over fear

life is about fun over fear.
if there's anything death has taught me,
get your proverbial shit in gear.

let me make it crystal clear:
live your life, write that novel, learn to ski!
life is about fun over fear.

i don't mean to sound insincere.
princess, you're not guaranteed that jubilee.
get your proverbial shit in gear.

travel and get that prized souvenir;
go to a karaoke bar and sing off-key.
life is about fun over fear.

before you say adieu and disappear,
try to live your life regret-free.
get your proverbial shit in gear.

we should make the most of it here;
unlock your comfort zone—you have a key.
life is about fun over fear!
get your proverbial shit in gear.

coin toss

Gratitude and Grief,
two sides of the same coin.
sisters who serve Love.

living is a privilege

life is an honor.
living is a privilege.
so, do more than breathe.

pulling the push door

thank goodness for friends
who get the enormity
of the big exit.

you've changed

exhausted, fire-fanged.
your you-ness will return soon,
even though you've changed.

later

it's seven months later.
Dad keeps busy and basks in your smile.
your youngest shines as woman and mother.
your granddaughter evolves and thrives.
your eldest tends a library in your honor.
your brother wishes for another vacation together.
your friends hold you fondly in their
memories.

you continue to walk among us.
your presence is tangible.

jacked up

i got a flat tire
on this trip around the sun.
i'm using the spare
to continue on my way,
and embrace what is out there.

notions of next

i have no notions of next.
it's pointless to be perplexed.
i choose to revel in the possibilities.

the kids are okay(ish)

Grief and Gratitude
regard each of us and say,
you are okay-ish.
it will take a lot of time
before the *ish* goes away.

giddy-up!

there were
     places you
          wanted to go.
            Tuscany.
              Egypt.
                on a safari.
              i'll try to
          continue the
        journey for you.
     where to
next?

saucy centennial

i want you to know
if i live to 100,
there *will* be stories.

the attack of the what-ifs

here's what the tarot cards told me:
prophetic messages on display.
reframing the what-ifs will set you free.

loud and clear—cards one, two, three!
trust your ideas—don't delay.
here's what the tarot cards told me:

things aren't always crappy.
the skies aren't always gray.
reframing the what-ifs will set you free.

don't create a prison–you're the only detainee;
not everything contains foul play.
here's what the tarot cards told me:

quit the internal negativity.
give the can-dos some leeway.
reframing the what-ifs will set you free.

there's no big mystery.
it's now, not someday.
here's what the tarot cards told me:
reframing the what-ifs will set you free.

bravery starts with your name

have a little faith.
cast out your inhibitions.
tell us who you are.

the door is always open

come for a visit!
swing by anytime.
arrive unannounced
in a dream
          on an airstream
                    while i daydream.

don't judge the house though.

k, thx.

until next time.

afterword

I visit the sisters' home regularly, and appreciate what Grief and Gratitude have taught me. Loss isn't a *one-stop-all-better-thanks-I'll-leave-a-five-star-review* kind of experience. It's okay to be sad. It's okay to be angry. It's okay to smile. It's okay to cry. It's okay to be loud. It's okay to be quiet. It's okay to question your own mortality. It's okay to say your loved ones' names.

I've learned to be kind to myself. If you're grieving someone, I hope you'll be kind to yourself, too.

A little kindness goes a long way. Donations to organizations fighting the good fights keep memories and hope alive—I'd like to highlight two:

- My Mom, above all things, loved her family— especially her children and grandchild. Consider donating to St. Jude's Children's Research Hospital. (stjude.org)

- Pancreatic cancer robbed my family and her friends of my Mom, and robs so many other families of their loved ones. I learned a lot from the Pancreatic Cancer Action Network. (pancan.org)

acknowledgments

Thank you, dear readers, for giving this collection and the sisters a chance.

A very special thanks to project management and proofreading guru, Bel Thresher, the uber-talented illustrator, Olivia L. Sutton, and to editor and poet extraordinaire, Shelby Leigh.

I am grateful for friends and supporters: Michelle Vitali, Eileen Grimes, Amy McCole, Todd Johnson, Lauren Palmer, Gabrielle Bilotta, Courtney O'Connor, Julie Shaw, and Tami Osborne.

Love and gratitude to my family, especially my Dad, my sister, my niece, and cousin Jim.

Thank you to my husband, Tito.

Finally, I am grateful for my Mom. She read everything I ever wrote. I hope she knows how much we love and miss her.

about the author

Cheryl Cantafio is an information technology professional and podcast co-host (*You Only Go Once (Y.O.G.O.)*. This is her debut as an author and poet. She lives in the suburbs of Philadelphia, Pennsylvania with her husband and their two mischievous mini-dachshunds. Connect with her on Instagram, @cherylc.writer

about the illustrator, editor, & project management

Illustrator

Olivia L. Sutton is a sophomore art student studying illustration and creative writing at PennWest Edinboro University. She hopes to work in publication and help herself and others share stories through art and writing. Connect with her on Instagram, @livbyart2001

Editor

Shelby Leigh is a self-love advocate, poetry editor, and author of three books, including the bestselling *changing with the tides*. She has worked with more than 100 poets to help them publish poetry collections. Connect with her on Instagram, @shelbyleighpoetry

Project Management and Proofreading

Abella Publishing Services, LLC provides publishers and authors all forms of publishing services from manuscript through bound/digital book, including editorial, design, indexing, and project management. They make the process of publishing books simpler. Connect with them on the web, https://www.abellaps.com

CPSIA information can be obtained
at www.ICGtesting.com
Printed in the USA
BVHW091938130423
662312BV00016B/211